Father of The Bride Wedding Speech

How to Deliver Impressive & Awesome Wedding Speeches

LUNA PEARL

Copyright © 2020 Luna Pearl

All rights reserved.

ISBN: 978-1-71693-390-5

CONTENTS

1 THE D-DAY IS HERE, FINALLY 1
2 IMPORTANT POINTS OF THE FATHER OF THE BRIDE SPEECH DIFFERENT FROM OTHER SPEECHES 4
3 THE ESSENCE OF THE SPEECH 7
4 YOUR ROLE AS THE FATHER OF THE BRIDE IN THE WEDDING CEREMONY 9
5 NICE SAMPLE SPEECHES 11
8 SHOW YOUR AFFECTION 20
9 DON'T FORGET THESE LITTLE THINGS 23
10 WARM TEARS IN YOUR EYES 27
11 BEHAVE YOURSELF AND YOUR BODY ETIQUETTE 32
12 A TEMPLATE TO MAKE YOUR LIFE EASIER 35
13 PREPARE YOURSELF TO WRITE 38
14 DON'T FORGET YOUR DUTY 43
15 SECRTES INGREDIENTS 46
16 YOU ARE THE HOST OR MC 48
17 IDEAS FOR YOUR SPEECH 50
18 YOU ARE READY TO ROCK AND ROLL 54

1 THE D-DAY IS HERE, FINALLY

The wedding day is here, finally. Your little darling is getting married, and there is a lot going on in your mind right now, isn't it? Mixed emotions, you are happy and a bit sad at the same time. Well, after all, why wouldn't you have these emotions running up and down in you, after all, your little angels' flying away to another nest from today for a completely new life, without your protection, care, and comfort, which you have been providing her so far.

To make things simpler for you today and for the special occasion, this Book has everything from general guidelines to do's and don'ts to etiquettes to sample speeches. As the Father of the Bride all you've got to do is to look gorgeous, not that you are not one hell of a handsome stallion even at this age, however, a little polishing and touch-up's here and there would only make your inner hidden personality come out, O yes, don't forget the name of your to be son-in-law!

As a father your little girl now ready for marriage and a new life has always been looking at you for courage, strength, love, and guidance. While mothers have been a source of strength for all grooms, the fathers have always been the hero for their daughters, hence the phrase has been rightly coined " Daddy's little girl", and if you are a hero, you better act like one honey, because there are certainly no two ways about it, especially at your darling angel's wedding.

So shed away all those nervous feelings and ignore the flying butterflies.

Your job on this big day is to happily hand over your daughter's hand in marriage to an able and deserving son-in-law. This E-Book aims at providing you with solutions for the perfect speech for your little angel. Some of the aspects covered in this E-Book are speech samples, body etiquette, overcoming your emotions, and other related issues. It also includes guidelines on making an apt speech, which would make your daughter proud of her strong daddy dearest.

Whether you are an eloquent speaker or an amateur, this E-Book provides you amazing insight on how to begin, what to include, humorous one-liners, and icebreakers. You will be amazed at how the book brings out the best in you, no matter what style is.

Then again, whether you are a writer or want to stay miles away from the job, you would find this e-book handy. In addition, do peek at the sample speeches section. This is the area where you could harvest enough ideas to start your own research and planning.

Like all important things in life, your daughter's wedding needs pre-planning and adequate preparation. Sometimes it is better to start planning months before the event so that you are well prepared. While going through the various sections of this E-Book, you will notice that you are preparing yourself as an individual for a grand celebration, well in advance.

A wedding ceremony is incomplete without wedding speeches and toasts. Wedding speeches form a part of the many traditions that a wedding ceremony must follow. Though it has been mandatory for the men to make all the wedding speeches on the D-day, these days even brides and brides maid's go on to give their wedding speeches. The first one to start a series of wedding speeches in a traditional wedding ceremony is always the father of the bride.

The father of the bride raises a toast to the newlyweds and guests and gives his speech which is followed by the groom who must thank him for opening the wedding speeches at the wedding ceremony. Writing a father of the bride wedding speech is not as difficult as it seems though. A little research and creativity can land you with a father of the bride wedding speech that is sure to leave everyone with a smile on their faces. A winning shot at the wedding of your darling angel assured.

Remember, that the father is the pillar of strength and a source of constant guidance for the bride. It is therefore of particular importance on how he conducts himself before and after the ceremony; how he mingles with the crowd; how he addresses the gathering. In a nutshell, everything, just everything to make the grand wedding grander can be done with the help of a simple speech.

One thing that you need to do here is to imagine Steve Martin in the classic movie 'Father of the Bride' and you would realize how much you could empathize with that character. However, it is the day when your darling would be waiting to put her arms around you after the speech, and cry tears of joy. The emotions of happiness and parting have to be merged in an ecstatic combination in the speech.

2 IMPORTANT POINTS OF THE FATHER OF THE BRIDE SPEECH DIFFERENT FROM OTHER SPEECHES

One of the unique things about weddings is that the speech givers hold a very special bond with either the bride or the groom. Hence, what they are going to say is going to be a vital part of memories to be remembered for a long time.

However, the love and the bond that a daughter and a father share is something that cannot be described in words. Psychologically speaking the speech of the father is always biased towards the bride, and there is a tinge of jealousy because the groom is taking away his most prized possession.

Therefore, when you are writing a speech for your daughter's wedding you should remember that there should be no sarcastic comments or biased comments towards the groom. You should be happy for the couple and try to portray your emotions in a positive way for the sake of your daughter. The wedding speech would be largely on your emotions for your daughter and letting her know how happy you are.

Hence, when you sit down to plan your speech you should think of it in a positive way, and picture it with a smile on your face. You should have faith in your daughter's choice and give the speech with confidence. Before you speak, you should completely forget the fact that your daughter would be parting you or what lies ahead.

While making the speech your focus should be to enjoy yourself and take everything in only at the moment. The end of the speech is probably the worst because here you would be bidding farewell to your daughter. The emotions of not seeing her when you get back home or not being able to wake her every morning start dawning on you.

Therefore, the end of the speech has to be something outstanding and you should try to add humorous or funny content at the end. The idea is that you should be picturing it with everyone applauding and imagining them laughing. One can find some humorous wedding speech jokes about the bride from the father, which can be used in this context.

As the father of the bride, you should remember that before you stand up for making the speech you should avoid looking nervous. Rather you should be composed and confident so that others cite you as an example. Try to think of the happy times that you spent with your daughter.

It is also very common for the father and the daughter to have tears in their eyes during the ceremony. Allow the tears to come with a smile so that you can give your little darling some consolation and help her to smile too.

As the speech begins, it is best for you to glance around the guests present in the marriage ceremony. This would also help you to make eye contact with them and helps the speaker to relax with an air of confidence. Do not worry about the requirements at the wedding reception while you are making the speech.

It is best to leave someone in charge of the reception ceremony while you are making the speech or attending the toasts of the other guests. To relax a little during the toasting process you should ask to have a non-alcoholic beverage so that you can remain composed, and the throat does not become very dry.

Many fathers have a certain kind of fear regarding public speaking, especially on the wedding day of their daughters. Hence, this makes giving a wedding speech all the more difficult. However, you should try to picture your daughter and her childhood memories right before the ceremony so that you are in a good mode and are able to make the speech without getting nervous.

3 THE ESSENCE OF THE SPEECH

All weddings have different kinds of themes and traditions, but most weddings have a basic format that remains common. There is no doubt that wedding speeches are important in any wedding ceremony as they serve not just as formalities but also add insight to the bride and groom. The speeches are there to bring out the real essence of the union that has been established.

The wedding speeches that are given by the father of the bride are amongst the most touching. During the wedding speech by the father of the bride, there is a need for content to be about both families and impersonal. The only exceptions here are given to the best man and maid of honor, who can insert more personal comments in their speeches.

Generally, the bride's father gives the first wedding speech and it is a tradition that if there is no master of ceremonies, who is also known as the toastmaster, then the father of the bride is to be introduced by the best man. During the speech, the father of the bride starts his speech by welcoming the guests to the wedding. The father of the bride is also the host of the wedding and thus it is vital that he thanks them for their attendance at the wedding of his daughter and her new husband.

The speech can be followed by talking about his daughter and here some of the memories of her temperament, babyhood, accomplishments, and skills. After this, he can also talk about his son and law, and give the speech a more personal approach. The finale of the speech includes a toast to the bride and the groom with special thanks to all the guests, and of course the groom's family. Usually, the father of the bride's speech is followed by the groom's speech, but this is a tradition that varies largely.

When the father of the bride is planning the wedding reception speech, it should be remembered that there is no requirement for you to fully conform to tradition. Sure, the father of the bride's speech is usually expected to be serious and emotional but you can take a few cues from the best man and add some fun component to the speech.

There are variations in the speeches made by the father of the bride and humor is used for both the bride and the groom. It is vital to be yourself rather than allowing yourself to be bounded by traditions. Before commencing the wedding speech it is suggested that you have a chat with close friends of the bride and groom.

This is essential to know some key secrets about the groom and also how the couple met and other related details. The father is supposed to know his daughter the best but there is no harm in trying to find out some fun things that you can add on here. Ask your other children to help you with the speech and add some other details about the bride and the groom.

4 YOUR ROLE AS THE FATHER OF THE BRIDE IN THE WEDDING CEREMONY

Apart from giving the speech at your daughter's wedding, there are scores of other things that you have to be prepared for. It is best to prepare the speech in advance because once you are bogged down with wedding preparations and attending the guests, you would not get time to rehearse your speech.

One of the most vital roles of the father of the bride is preparing for the wedding events. There is a lot to be done in the pre-wedding planning, and the father is the person who would be writing the checks and scanning the credit cards. Many other things have to be taken care of here. These include talking to the caterers, bookings for the band and venue, decorations, accommodation of guests, hiring other help, and most importantly getting a tuxedo for you.

Walking down the aisle is an imperative part of being at your daughter's wedding. However, there is much more than a father is expected to do for making the wedding an optimistic and memorable experience. Most of the wedding reception preparations and even expenses are taken care of by the father of the bride.

It should be remembered that the wedding reception is the remuneration after all the work associated with the wedding. This reception would be the perfect time to reconcile with family members, meet your friends, and wish your daughter and her husband for their new life.

Therefore, when you have the responsibility to plan for and pay the bills making a speech is the last thing on the mind. However, there is a need for you to find ample time to say something at your daughter's wedding. The speech made by the father is something that all daughters look forward to.

The father of the bride wedding speech and toasts need to be unique and focused on the bride and groom. There are plenty of favorite wedding toasts available here that can be personalized with some memorable moments and then be presented to the bride and groom.

Apart from the speech the father is also given the duty of dancing with the bride. Therefore, you can be assured that you are hands are going to be full starting from the pre-planning and will not end even after the last guests leave. Instead of getting more nervous about all the things that you would have to do for your daughter's wedding, there is a need for you to focus on other aspects.

There are certain factors that can help you in easing out the pressure of giving the speech and this includes planning your speech in advance.

5 NICE SAMPLE SPEECHES

Here are a few sample speeches that can be personalized by the father and can be used for the ceremony. These are samples that can be elaborated by adding some family traditions or they can be used with quotes and jokes to lighten the mood of the wedding ceremony.

I raise a toast for my daughter and the man she has chosen as her life companion. As a father, I still sometimes doubted if this day would ever come, and sometimes feared what her choice would be like. However, today I am proud that my daughter has made the right choice. She is a princess to me and will always be. Here is a toast to my little girl, may all happiness and joy be with you.

I am here to raise glasses and toast the happy couple. The bride has always been like the ray of warm sunshine on my soul since she was born. In addition, as she begins a new life, with another man, to whom she will turn for love and safety, I can only say that I am proud of her choice. Nevertheless, I want her to know that I am always going to be there for her and I know that she will always be there for me.

Here's a toast to my daughter and her new husband. In addition, as you raise your glasses remember this truth that her lucky man and I have both gained something on this blessed day. He is gaining with a wife and a companion for life, and I am getting some new stack of bills to pay.

I lift my glass to honor my son in law on this day. I cannot express my happiness at my daughter's wedding and find it hard to find the right words. The depths of my feelings are best understood by her, and

all that I can say is that she was a fine daughter. I also know that she wills a fine wife too. As my thoughts are being filled with a curious mixture of joy and wonder, I wish the happy couple joy and happiness. I can see her eyes sparkle every time she looks at _____ and I still wonder at the miracle of seeing my baby child become a woman.

It is said that daughters are a gift from heaven, and for me, this was the best blessing that I could ever ask for. As I make a toast to my daughter I want to thank god for this beautiful gift and I will always be grateful to have her in my life. The honor of being her father has always been a blessing for me. Here's wishing that God continued to bless her and her new husband with love, and happiness for all the days of their lives.

As the father of the bride, you can also ask the bride and the groom for grandchildren.

For example, (Bride and Groom), here's wishing that the future brings you happiness, wisdom, and many children to make me a grandfather! I give you my wholehearted blessing and hope that the happy day also comes soon for you. Many congratulations to the two of you!

Another example here is- Every time I look at my daughter, the bride, I cannot help but mirror on all the years when I had been fortunate enough to watch her grow and emerge as the lovely woman she is today. She had my heart from the day she was born, and with each passing year, I only grew more in awe of her. I propose a toast for my little girl, my princess, and my darling, who will always remain the same for me, no matter how old she grows.

As I watch her marry a wonderful man I can just feel proud and confident that she and (Groom) would be embarking on a wonderful journey filled with love and happiness. I hope the two of you always treat each other with love and compassion, for all the years ahead. I ask you to join me today to congratulate the bride, groom and wish them for a long and happy life together.

During the speech, it is also vital for the father of the bride to add a few sentences about the groom. This is essential for him to express his happiness with the wedding. For instance, you can say that ___ is a fine man here and I am really happy that my daughter has chosen him.

6 POEMS TO MAKE THE WEDDING MEMORABLE

Apart from the regular speeches, the father of the bride can also include a few poems in the speech. These are poems that one can use to convey their heartiest feelings to their loved ones.

1. For example,

They say that coming together is a beginning,

Moreover, being together is in progress.

However, working together is a success.

Moreover, I wish the same for my daughter and son in law. ____ and ____ I just wish that your life together be just the starting of some of the glorious days of your life. There are going to be days when life can take many turns along the way. These are times when you will have your glory days and there will your sad days too. However, by having each other, you will have all that you need. The tools for a successful marriage are clinging to each other, communicating with each other, and making each other number the priority of your lives.

2. When I look at the bride and the groom all that I can say is-

Here's a toast to the past and for all that you have learned

Here's a toast for the present, for all the days that you are going to share

Moreover, here one for the future, for all that you look forward to together.

3. Let me introduce you with an ode to reality…

That would keep your marriage brimming,

With lots of love in the loving cup

Admit it whenever you're wrong

And whenever you are right, do shut up!

4. My little princess,

When I saw you come into this world,

So soft and tiny!

As I held you in my arms, I knew that it was love,

Watching you grow up and wiping your tears,

Seeing you laugh and play makes me realize how fast the years went by.

They seem like such short years now.

I just have one last task to do… Walking down the alley beside you.

It won't be easy to let go of you, and letting you go…

Is the hardest thing for me to do?

But I know that he loves you too, maybe more than me too.

I just want you to remember that I would always love you!

5. Here's a special toast for the bride so fair,

And here's to groom found so rare!

Here's to marriage, where two souls merge as one,

But most of all here's a toast to daddy's little darling…

The prettiest one!

6. Here's one to the prettiest of them all,

One for the wittiest and truest of all,

But most of all here's one to someone whose dad loves most of all!

7. Wishing that each petal on the shamrock

Brings a happy wish your way…

May good health, luck, and happiness,

Find you today and every day.

8. A healthy and long life to you.

Land, without worrying about rent…

A child to love and care,

Here's a toast to a lovely daughter,

Remember that I would always be there.

7 DON'T MISS OUT HILARIOUS JOKES

There is a general connotation that the father of the bride speech has to be something serious and emotional. But there are times when you can always lighten the mood of the wedding by adding some quick jokes. You can be the conventional father who loves to crack jokes and welcome the son in law to your house.

The wedding speeches are focused on wishing the bride and groom many good things on their special day. But the fun element is also essential in the speech so that you can say goodbye to your little darling with a smile on her face.

Humor should be a part of any good father of the bride's speech and hence it is vital to include jokes and make it funny. Even though it may sound easy, using humor is not really that simple for the father. One of the many reasons for the same is that you cannot help but think that your daughter would be going away very soon.

And, as the host for the evening and the father of the bride, it is vital not to offend anyone in your speech. More importantly, the humor used should not be excessively focusing on embarrassing anyone, especially the groom. You have to maintain subtle humor here, as you are the father of the bride.

There are many things that you can use here for making jokes and this includes some family traditions. Some of the people you can make fun of including your family in general. For example, you can say about some very funny habit of the bride as a child or how she hated getting a haircut.

You can also crack a joke about how un-functional your family is or how they can do weird things that make others giggle. Then there are certain elements about the bride, that you can mention here, especially stories from her childhood.

One of the most important factors to remember here is that you should not lecture about how you warned her against dating some horrid men. Rather say that you are really happy that the bride chose the groom because he is a kind-hearted and loving person.

Remember that the groom is also expected to be in the speech and as the bride's father you can also make a joke or two about the groom. However, it has to be kept in mind that you should keep it light-hearted. In the wedding speech, you can talk about some mishaps that happened earlier in the day. Or even talk about something funny that happened during the wedding ceremony.

If your daughter had been fond of shopping then you can say that ____ (groom) it is time now that I warned you about your credit card bills, which are certainly going to grow in leaps and bounds.

____ (bride) if you are right then fighting for it if you are wrong then fight for it all the more, just like your mother does.

____ (groom) there are only two times in a man's life when he fails to understand a woman, before and after marriage.

After this, you should try to finish off on a happier note and mention that you are really happy for the couple. Remember that you can crack a few jokes about the groom's parents too if you have known them for a while. All jokes directed at the parents of the grooms should be sober and subtle. You can also crack jokes on behalf of the entire family like warning the groom about how long his bills would be or taking tips for handling her temper from our family.

8 SHOW YOUR AFFECTION

Weddings in the family or among close friends are very important occasions, where best efforts are usually taken to make the event as hassle-free and memorable as possible. There's no doubt that the parents or close friends of a person go that extra length to make the ceremony outstanding – a happening that not just the neighborhood but the whole town would talk about for years to come.

Ever since the day she was born, the daughter is a proud part of the family, on equal footing as the son. In the case of a father, the attachment towards a daughter is usually much more than that towards a son. The daughter too is generally more attached to the father than the mother in an average household. The love and care given are reflected right from the dolls and toys given to her in her childhood to the quality of education and opportunities offered as she grows.

Speeches delivered on such occasions can vary. They can be serious, packed with tear-jerking feelings, they could be matter-of-fact and pragmatic or they could be jovial and lighthearted, but with good intent. Or, they could be a mix of all three moods.

A meaningful and memorable speech could strike a balance – give rise to emotion, make the gathering laugh and yet, at the same time, carry enough weight so that lines (at least one or two) can be quoted by others in the future. Ideally, they should not belong for, unlike politicians, the use of rhetoric is limited. Besides, the possibility of deterioration in the standard of delivery is more if the speech is more. The length of a good speech should be within five minutes.

There are a lot of problems that you can be experimenting with currently like trying to be in compliance with the wishes of the organizers, be he or she a best friend, the mother, or the father of the bride or groom, especially the bride. But there may be several constraints the organizers have to overcome in order to carry out this wish. These are usually in the form of finances, organizational capabilities, and time, most of all time.

For a working person already bogged down by business or office commitments, arranging a daughter's wedding is no simple task. From deciding on what scale to have the ceremony and the guest list to the venue for the reception, the decorations, the wedding gown, the design of the cake, the menu, the wines…the decisions and actions to be taken are endless.

This is also why in today's busy world; adopting a division of responsibility is a wise move. Taking up the execution of every little thing is an imprudent policy, which could result in all the attempts to make the occasion a grand success ending up in grand failure. There are ways out. A worried father could hire the services of a wedding planner so that he is not bogged down with work. The underlying factor, either way, is the trust and faith one has in the path one takes. People usually rely on time-tested practices and on what they had gone through and seen at the time of their wedding.

There can be different situations where a father has to give his speech at his daughter's wedding. One could be where she is the only child or the only daughter, whereby the words tend to be more power-packed and emotional. Or the daughter could be challenged in some way and the groom is willing to take her responsibility. In another situation, the daughter could have decided to take the plunge after years of contemplation. Each situation has different content and approach. Some samples are appended.

As the father of the bride, all the emotions that a daughter might be experiencing at that point in time should be taken into consideration. But most importantly, she would be looking forward to hearing some encouraging words from you. Remember that even though your darling is all grown up now, she still needs your finger to take that final step.

9 DON'T FORGET THESE LITTLE THINGS

There are two ways of writing a great father of the bride wedding speech. Either you can make it formal and really emotional, or you can make it light-hearted, yet nice with a dash of humor to make everyone smile, especially your daughter who would be leaving your home for a new life forever. Your content would solely depend on the audience that you would be addressing. The best way to begin your father of the bride wedding speech is to open with wishes for the newlyweds and a welcome note to all the guests present at the wedding ceremony.

Remember most of the guests present at the wedding ceremony are most likely not known to you. There will be quite a few people from the groom's side whom you, as the father of the bride, will be meeting for the first time. Thus, it becomes really important for you to introduce yourself to the wedding guests present in the opening lines of your wedding speech so that everyone is well acquainted with you. Once you have completed with the opening lines of your father of the bride wedding speech, with the welcome notes, wishes and introductions, move on to the body of your wedding speech.

The body of your father of the bride wedding speech can be written really innovatively and creatively. If the mood of the ceremony is light-hearted and not too conservative it would be best to throw in some humor and jokes into your wedding speech. One of the best ways to get your wedding speech moving is to speak about the first day you met your son in law with a dash of humor, you could also go on related any particular incident in reference to the planning of the wedding ceremony that could get everyone laughing!

The jovial mood is best for a wedding ceremony. Once you have lightened the mood of the audience you can proceed to address your daughter. Remember, it is a very sentimental event for her, especially because daughters are more attached to their fathers, your speech will surely bring tears to her eyes. So be careful of the words you choose to address her in your wedding speech.

The words should be emotional, stressing on the beautiful bond you both share as father and daughter, but should not leave her heavy-hearted. You can bring in childhood memories from the day she was born. You can say, "We can never forget the day, a little angel came into our lives… I can't imagine that my little angel has grown up into such a beautiful and wonderful person so quickly… And today she stands before us as a bride. How time flies…

While you proceed further with your father of the bride wedding speech, dedicate a considerable part of your speech to your daughter… The bride. You can put in her little childhood acts, funny incidents that you both shared, holidays you went to as a family, her first day in school, her friends, her college days, her teen tantrums, just about anything to emphasize upon the wonderful relationship you both share.

Don't forget to speak about your daughter's accomplishments be it in school, college, or life. You can mention awards won by her, and how happy you were when she brought those awards home to you. Her first job, if she is working. Appreciate and compliment her, even if you have never done that before. Girlie stories about your daughter can really lighten the mood of your father of the bride wedding speech. Just be careful that you don't hurt your daughter's sentiments. Don't insult her in any way; rather hold her up in high esteem.

Emphasize on factors that make you proud to be called her father. You can also share your experiences of bringing your daughter up from childhood to present. Don't forget to mention your wife and the wonderful job that she has done in bringing up your daughter from a sweet little child to a dignified young woman.

You can also include stories about some tough situations that your daughter has handled single-handedly in life. If she has done some acts of bravery, this is your opportunity to make the world know. Whatever you do, just be careful not to mention your daughter's suitors or ex-boyfriends, or for that matter of fact anything that would otherwise embarrass her publicly.

End your father of the bride wedding speech with a note of thanks to all the guests present and for the blessings that they have showered on your daughter on her special day. Let your daughter and your son in law know through the concluding lines of your father of the bride wedding speech, how happy you are to see them married and that you wish them a wonderful life ahead. Appreciate your son in law for being the wonderful man he is, this will only strengthen your relationship with your son in law and your daughters-in-law.

Your wedding speech as the father of the bride must end with a toast raised to the newlyweds wishing them a happy life together and the guests present to grace the wedding ceremony of your daughter from near and far. You can add in wedding jokes or quotes too in your speech to lighten the mood of the audience. Stories about your daughter breaking the news of her wedding to you or your first meeting with your son in law is a must for every father of the bride wedding speeches.

While putting in humor and jokes into your speech don't include lines that may hurt your daughter. Use light humor like "(Daughter's name) I don't want you to get emotional and cry as your cake is already in tiers!" It's sure to make your daughter and everyone laugh out! You can add stories about your own wedding into your speech with quotes like "Marriage is like wine - It gets better with age." and refer to how wonderful and experience it has been for you even to this day to be married to the bride's mother.

Stories of lasting romances surely have an impact on newlyweds who are in an anxious state of mind on how their relationship will turn out to be. Romantic, real-life, long-lasting matrimonial stories only boost their confidence levels. You can also add in a bit of advice to the newlyweds on how delicate the bond of marriage is and how they both must stand by each other in good times and bad to strengthen the beautiful bond that they share.

Keep a glass of champagne in hand for the toasts you will be raising through your father of the bride wedding speech and also keep a glass of water in hand to soak your throat. Be confident, relaxed, and at ease with your speech. Keep your speech short and crisp yet emotional. Your speech as the father of the bride is important as it will set the mood for many other speeches to follow and will also get the wedding reception rolling.

There are numerous websites that provide sample wedding speeches for the father of the bride, do look them up before you sit down to chalk out your father of the bride speech, as they are bound to provide you with proper guidance. Conclude your wedding speech with a note of thanks to everyone who made this wedding day a memorable affair for you and your family and even the wedding planner for that matter of fact. It's sure to make an impression on everyone present especially your daughter who would be emotionally moved by your speech. Go ahead make your father of the bride speech memorable, it's a great way to welcome your son in law into your family and lives. Good luck!

10 WARM TEARS IN YOUR EYES

Traditionally it is the father of the bride who begins the series wedding speeches at a wedding reception, followed by the groom and best man. Your father of the bride's speech may seem difficult to pin down but it's not very tough, especially, because the father of the bride is the best person to speak about his daughter. You have seen her grow from a little child to an elegant woman.

Express your emotions with warmth and depth. There are certain emotions that you must include in your father of the bride speech while delivering the same. This chapter is to guide you in including these particular emotions in your father of the bride wedding speech that would make your daughter's wedding speech really special and memorable.

The opening lines of your father of the bride wedding speech must begin with a note of thanks to all your friends and family members who have come to bless your daughter and son in law on this special occasion. An important note of thanks must be kept aside for anyone who has helped you organize the wedding and got things together to make this day all the more special for us.

Say thank you to your daughter for being a wonderful daughter to you and bringing so much happiness in your life. Let your daughter and son in law know how proud you are of them. It is an emotional situation to see your daughter move on to a new life out of your nest. Express your love to her even if you have never done so openly as a father on her special day. Speak about her childhood, the silly things she might have done. It's sure to make everyone smile.

If you are planning to add a dash of humor into your father of the bride wedding speech, make sure it's light-hearted and doesn't hurt someone's feeling. For-ex, you can say, "Thank you, everyone, for being here to bless (daughter and son in laws name) on this joyous occasion. This day will surely be memorable for me, especially I am thinking about the time when the bride and the groom run out of here after presenting the bill of the ceremony to me!" Or you can keep it really formal like "Thank you, everyone, for being here with us on this special day."

As you move on to the body of your father of the bride wedding speech, talk about your daughter's childhood, her first day at school., go on to speak about the experiences that you have had bringing up your daughter. Go on, and speak about your family vacations, any funny incident, and then let everyone know about your first meeting with your son in law.

You can even add in any humorous events that may have happened during the courtship years of your daughter, that could get everyone laughing, though don't do anything to embarrass the bride and the groom. You can also share stories about the first day you met your son in law and your first meeting with your son-in-law's family. It's sure to create a bond between the two families. Appreciating your daughter's in-laws in your father of the bride wedding speech as it is a great way to create an impression on them.

After your daughter and in-laws, it is your chance to dedicate a part of your speech as the father of the bride to your son in law. You can talk about the first time you met him, were there any funny incidents involved in your first meeting with him, the way your relationship developed, what made you agree in giving your daughter's hand in marriage to your son in law, what are the qualities about him that touched your heart and made you say yes to the relationship.

Share it all here. You can even include the excitement and fun you had planning your daughter's wedding until the D-day. End off by letting your daughter and son in law know that, "I am the luckiest to have an understanding, loving and caring daughter like you in my life and now I have a bonus, a wonderful son in law too!.".

While complimenting your son in law, sound as genuine as possible. Speak from your heart... Include wedding quotes. Add phrases like "Made for each other", "Dream comes true", "made for each other". Do everything you can through your words to make your son in law feel special. Make him know how happy you are to have him as your son in law, and how much you are looking forward to his daughter settling down with him, for a bright and happy future ahead.

End off your father of the bride wedding speech with a special note of thanks to all your guests, family, friends and associates as well as your wedding planner, hairdresser or designer for that matter of fact, and all those who have made your daughter's special day all the more special for you and your family and raise a toast to all those concerned. Thank your guests for the gifts they have given to your daughter and son in law.

Thank the priest, congregation, or any church minister who has been a part of your daughter's wedding ceremony and vows. Let everyone know how happy you are with the overall wedding ceremony and that everything would not have turned out just the way you and your daughter had dreamt and planned without the support of some people. Don't forget to mention a special thank you to your wife for her constant support and her role in bringing up your daughter.

Just a note... There may be some special circumstances during which your wedding has taken place. There could have been a sudden death in the family, or someone really close may not have been able to be by your side on your D-Day. It would be wonderful if you could mention the same in your wedding speech. It will surely touch the heart of all those present. For a deceased family member, you could say... "It saddens me to not have (aunt Anne-name of deceased) with us on our special day, but I am sure he is blessing us from up above. May his soul rest in peace?"

Apart from that if there's a missing relative, a friend who could not make it or children who missed the occasion for school exams, do put in a word for them. Whatever you do don't mention your daughter's ex-boyfriends, ex-husbands, or crushes! Don't hurt anyone's feelings. Just be natural, be yourself, and express your gratitude to all your wedding guests through your bride's wedding speech.

Leave a lasting impression on everyone present at your wedding especially your daughter and son in law; after all, he must realize how lucky he is to now be associated with your daughter and her family. As you are the father of the bride not many people would know you, so use this opportunity to introduce yourself to everyone and create a lasting impression as you do so.

Give your opinion on how happy you are to see your daughter married to the man of her dreams. Add stories and wedding quotes. They are bound to make an impact. Express all happiness that your daughter has ever brought to you, right from her birth to her achievements in school or college life, any special competitions that she has won, if she was working, and her first job offer. This is your opportunity to make her feel really special and loved on her wedding day. She will definitely miss you a whole lot once she is away. Let her know what she means to you.

Just don't be nervous, be calm and poised and most of all to be yourself as you give your wedding speech... Let all your friends and family know what a wonderful experience it has been in bringing you up to your daughter, highlight her achievements and let everyone know how proud and happy you are to see her as a beautiful bride that she is today. Make your father of the bride's wedding speech as emotional and personal as you can. Touch the heart of the present and associated with your wedding through your bride's wedding speech. After all, you will be the first one to get a series of wedding speeches and toasts following!

11 BEHAVE YOURSELF AND YOUR BODY ETIQUETTE

It's your daughter's D-day and she is all set to start a whole new life with your wishes and blessings. Once the customs are traditions associated with your wedding, like the church affair, exchange of vows, etc. are over, it's time for the celebrations to begin... Your daughter's wedding reception. Traditionally, every wedding reception commences with wedding speeches, beginning with an emotional speech by the father of the bride. So, get it in your head that you will set the mood for the occasion. Introduce yourself with confidence as the "father of the bride."

Remember, your father of the bride wedding speech is a way to thank every one of your guests who have traveled wide and far to be here, your daughter's in-laws, friends, and relatives for all their support, so don't let this opportunity go. It is also a fabulous opportunity for you to display your love for your daughter before everyone. She will love it. Let everyone know how happy you are for your daughter and son in law, that you believe that they are both are made for each other and how lucky you are to have them in your life.

However, take note of this that just being ready with a well-written father of the bride's speech is not enough. There are certain body etiquettes that you must follow as the father of the bride while delivering your father of the bride's wedding speech, so that you grab the attention of all your guests, being the first one to start off the wedding speeches and also create an impression on your daughter's in-laws who will actually get to know your daughter and her family through you. So, make your introductions properly and try to sound confident!

Before you begin with the opening lines of your father of the bride wedding speech, make sure that you are not nervous and shaking. Cool down, drink a glass of water. Stand up when you deliver your speech as the father of the bride. Keep a glass of champagne in hand so that you can raise your toasts to the special people in concern like your daughter, the groom, your daughter's in-laws, whenever required in between your speech.

Keep a glass of water close by to soak your throat occasionally so that your word comes out loud and clear. Don't be conscious of your looks or your wedding suit. Don't get distracted by thinking about how you are looking. You are the father of the bride, make your mark! Just be comfortable with yourself as you deliver your wedding speech.

Begin your father of the bride's wedding speech with a thank you note to your guests. Sound emotional and let the words come out from your heart. You can say "Thank you (daughter's name)… I am here all because of you… You have made me a proud father and I am sure you will be a wonderful wife to (grooms name). Thank you for making this wedding day a memorable and special event." Go on to thank your in-laws for accepting your daughter. Thank your son in law. Appreciate his qualities and tell your daughter he is the best for her.

Don't scream and shout, talk softly. If you are uncomfortable with the mike, avoid it. Be presentable and deliver each word with grace and dignity like a man. Stand upright. Once you raise your toasts to wait for your guests to respond. End your wedding speech with a note of thanks to everyone and express yourself on how happy you are with the proceedings of the day. Be confident and keep smiling and you'll find yourself giving a memorable father of the bride's wedding speech that will be spoken about by one and all in the days to come, will make your daughter, son in law, your daughter's in-laws and your wife proud of you!

12 A TEMPLATE TO MAKE YOUR LIFE EASIER

"Good evening everyone. You all can't imagine how special a day this is for me. Not just because my daughter is marrying the man of her dreams but also because we have all you wonderful people here with us on this special day to celebrate and add to our joys. (Your wife's name) and I am really happy to have you all and want to thank you all for your gracious presence in this joyous ceremony. This day will be a memorable one for us all our lives.

Firstly, I want to thank you (daughter's name) for being such a wonderful daughter…From feeding you in a bottle to helping you choose my wedding gown it has been a wonderful experience for me. I wonder what life would have been like had you not been there. Next, I want to thank you *(groom's name)* for choosing my daughter's hand in marriage. Boy!

You are a lucky man. Thank you *(wife's name)* for all that you have done in bringing up a daughter as wonderful as our beautiful bride today. (Daughter and son in laws name), you both are simply made for each other, I knew that from the day I met you first (son in laws name) that you were a perfect match for my daughter. *(Here you can elaborate further with stories about your first meeting, any humorous incident, how you accepted their decision to marry).* Thank you *(in-laws names)* for accepting my daughter so graciously into your family. You all are wonderful people.

(In the body of your father of the bride wedding speech you can incorporate memories of your daughter growing up, amongst other things). Take a look at this…

"When (daughter's name) was a little girl she always dreamed about finding her prince charming! She dreamt about wearing that flowing white gown and getting lifted off her feet by her groom with all her friends and family showering their love and blessings on her can't believe it's all a dream come true for her and us today." (Appreciate your daughter for her caring ways, soft nature, and love for all. Don't let her down or embarrass her in any way. Speak in the positive.) (Daughter's name) has been a caring and loving daughter all her life. She has brought us so much happiness.

(Go on to speak about the proceedings to your wedding day. How you planned, who helped you all etc. and how happy you are with the proceedings. Address your son in law separately… You can say…

"David, I still remember the day I met you… *(Mention any incident; you can add a dash of humor or a wedding joke)* You have made a special difference to my daughter's life and ours and I am so happy she said …"I do" Saying yes to you is the best thing she has ever done. I am so glad I didn't have to kiss a frog to find my prince charming! I wish you both the best in life. Thank you both for filling our life with so much happiness. I want you to know that our blessings will always be with you.

If you plan to give a father of the bride's speech, which is light, hearted and not too formal, adding some wedding jokes and humor would be great.

(Lastly, end your father of the bride's wedding speech with a general thank you note to everyone for being present on this wedding day and making it a memorable affair. Raise a toast to all concerned before you sit down)

Thank you, everyone, for making this day so special for us. I will remember it all in my life. Jane *(wife's name)* and I are really lucky to have been blessed with friends and family like you. This day wouldn't have been possible without all your wishes and constant support. Thank You! As you end your toast make grounds for your son in law to give the grooms speech next.

Use these techniques to create a speech that would depict your emotions for your daughter, along with gratitude for those present in the ceremony.

13 PREPARE YOURSELF TO WRITE

Writing the father of the bride's speech is not that tough, as you are able to pen down all your emotions. This is easy and the prime reason is that you are able to take a look at your daughter and write what you see. The most convenient way to write a speech is when your daughter is doing things that she would do normally, every day. Like, play with kids, washing up, etc, so just look at her and get the inspiration. Watch her carefully, what is she doing or thinking, etc.

Just remember what is going on inside your head. For instance, are you happy or feeling proud? Whatever is the emotion, write down everything. After this, you must save all the information for writing your speech. Why this is required is because people often when writing, tend to go blank. So, if little notes are taken with all your feelings in them then remembering the experience becomes easier.

If you are the father of the bride, then while writing a speech for the occasion, you have to include a few good things. The first thing is to write is a bit about your daughter and her childhood. This could be inclusive of a story or something but keep in mind that you are there to speak about the bride, your daughter. So, don't cause her any humiliation, you can joke a bit but see that she is not hurt in the process. You can talk about her school days, working days, or even when she was a little baby. These points are always good to be included in your speech and for the groom's family to know more about their daughter-in-law. So, this, in fact, is an ice-breaking moment.

Secondly, you can write about how she was prior to meeting her husband. For example, was she more confident than the present, happy, or reserved before than now? How she has turned out to be now after finding the perfect person for her.

This can be like an insight that people would know how great together they are. Finally and an important point to be included in the speech is how you feel about your daughter and vice versa. Start off by writing how you felt when she was a kid, whether she was good academically, or was she an athlete. Cite all these as examples in your speech. Then shift your speech to the present day scenario and how you feel about her and after giving her to her newly married husband.

All these are basic points that you are required to write in your speech as the father of the bride. In totality, you must round up your speech in not more than 1000 words or so. More than these words would really put off the guests and all those who would be present at the wedding reception. Follow all the basic guidelines given below and write a fluent and easy speech for yourself.

- Introduction. This should be with a small hi; welcome and thanks for coming would be in the beginning. Don't forget to give a quick introduction about yourself.

- Talk things about your daughter, as mentioned above, for example, a story, etc.

- Then talk about what she is like and how did she meet the groom and how has her life changed ever since.

- Speak about your feelings, taking the points mentioned above.

- And in the final part of your speech just thank all and raise a toast to the newlyweds.

As per the tradition, a father of the bride speech is the most anticipated one. This one is always a moment of emotions that is touching and heartiest. It is a part of the tradition for the bride's father to address all present, guests, family, etc and give thanks to all for attending and participating in his daughter's most important day. Then he has to raise a toast to her and his new son-in-law, wishing and giving his blessings to them for a happy married and blissful future together.

(a) The opening of your speech as a father of the bride should begin with thanking all your guests for their attendance on this beautiful and joyous day of your life. And also give your gratitude for sharing this joyous day with you and your family. You can also acknowledge some special people and their presence, for example, elders, people who traveled from far to be there, etc.

(b) Give compliments to your daughter; tell her how beautiful and angelic she looks. Let her know how proud you feel for her. If you feel like, share a simple and short story, depicting her childhood days or her relations in relation to her marriage, etc. But be cautious not to tell stories about her old relationships, like her ex-boyfriend or anything that would cause her embarrassment.

(c) Welcome the groom to your family as your new son-in-law. This is the official moment to make your daughter's groom your family's part, publicly. Give compliments to him too and tell how you think he is the daughter's best choice ever! This way, the groom would feel accepted and delighted at the same time.

(d) Now raise a toast with the glass and lead a toast directed to the newly wedded.

(e) Write short notes, so that you are able to remember some of the main points in the speech. In spite of all the preparation and rehearsals, you still can become nervous and have jitters on this special occasion and require some assistance too.

Write and be prepared to give a father of the bride speech in the most confident, yet with emotions and sentiments. After all, you are the proud father of the bride and you have to maintain that too till the end. Accept your son-in-law with open arms and even you don't, try to be as welcoming as you can be. But don't go overboard, as it would be visible through your speech. Avoid sarcasm and overtly good attitude that too would show.

Preparation: Speeches are amongst the best part of a wedding tradition and reception. Being the father of the bride, it's your honor and duty to deliver the first speech. This can be a moment of intimidation, especially if you are not into public addressing or giving speeches in public. But there is another truth, some people are dreaded to speak in public, they have the fear of getting embarrassed in public and in front of many people. If you are on such an individual having fears and anticipation, then you can learn to speak and deliver a speech.

Simply, follow the advice given below and prepare the father of the bride speech. This way, on a real day, you would be flawless and give the perfect speech as the father of the bride.

The most vital key to the success of speech deliverance lies mostly in preparation of one and also in practice, till you are able to internalize it and are also able to speak without any kind of hesitation and naturally. If your content is good and has a proper practice then you would be more confident and feel great in giving your speech, as the father of the bride.

There should be a proper structure for your speech, beginning with the start, the middle, and the end to it. Avoid providing too much of content, apart from this, the speech is yours. Therefore, it is completely up to you and it is your freedom to say whatever you want to. Keep a check, whether the bride and groom want to say anything or not.

Traditionally, speeches at the wedding reception are given after dinner but time is not a criterion. So, you should better check on your preparation. If you visit the venue then you can get a lot of help in the preparation. This is because; you would know your location, the room's size. Another thing would help a lot if you know the number of guests expected to be present and if possible, know little things about them, thereby being able to tailor the speech according to them too.

Limit your speech, don't let it become long. This way you would not lose on the attention of your guests. Aim at around 5 to 10 minutes of speech time. If it so happens, that it becomes shorter than this then there is no need to worry. The reason is that you would at least have something to speak, which counts more than anything.

14 DON'T FORGET YOUR DUTY

Your task as the father of the bride is not restricted to having fun alone. Apart from the duties at the wedding, preparing the speech for your little darling is also important.

The speech of the best man is the most common one in a wedding reception. But the groom and also the father of the bride deliver a speech too. The speech made by the father of the bride would be his introduction as the host of the evening or also an acknowledgment made to the hosts by him. It provides if with an opportunity to honor and thank all, who have been involved in the special occasion, from the bride's party to the minister, who had married his daughter to her new husband.

There are no traditions or rules that dictate whether a speech should be a lighthearted or a serious one. But if you are the father of the bride, then you are expected to be solemn and subtle in giving your speech unlike the tribute made by the best man.

Thank you: Speech made by the father of the bride, allows him to greet all guests to the wedding reception and also thank them for their honorable presence. Along with this, he gives thank you for all the gifts brought by the guests. The father also gives thanks via his speech to all the people who had played an important role in putting the wedding together and other events related to it. After wrapping up his speech, the father also gives his blessings to the newly wedded couple and also gives acknowledgment to the mother of the bride or his own wife, showing gratitude for the years that they have shared as a couple together.

Welcome: Father of the bride through his speech, lend a welcoming arm to his new son-in-law, that to his family and along with him his family too. The father should talk about the groom's qualities that he admires and the reason why he feels that he is the best match and the best person meant for his daughter, the bride. He should say about his happiness and feelings, of his daughter finding such a worthy partner to share her entire life.

Daughter: In his speech, a father is able to express his love and emotion for his daughter. And also tell her how much she means and matters to him and the family. He would tell all the guests and people present on that day about his daughter's good qualities and character. He also talks about watching her grow up into a beautiful woman and a bride too.

Advice: Speech is the apt time for a father to extend all the advice and solemn or playful, related to his experience in marital life, of joys and demands, etc. The guidance given by him is very significant, in spite of his daughter being a mature woman and having all the sense. It still signifies that the bond between a father and daughter would never end, or diminish. It also shows how important a role he plays, and always will, in her life.

Recognition: This speech of the father of the bride is also a significant moment to pay tribute to various milestones signifying the union between two souls and also between two families. It is the most appropriate time, for him to make an address to any strife that has been able to strengthen their relationship and also recognize all the accomplishments made recently.

Blessings and supports: Payment made for a wedding is support in itself but the speech also gives an opportunity to the father to state publicly that his support would always be there for the couple and he, along with his family would be there for assisting and guiding them through their married life. The closing of the speech is made by the father raising a toast, congratulation, and giving all his blessings to the couple. He can also recite or read a prayer for their future.

15 SECRTES INGREDIENTS

A wedding is completely filled with joy, love, tears, and laughter. This the day is complete with magical moments and there is something really mesmerizing, so much so that callous of callous person has a good time, parties and laugh all through the night! Romance might be the reason for such changes and also because of the company that is brought only during weddings. Maybe it is an ultimate feminine feeling, with so many beautiful looking women in their lovely outfits and also the men looking dazzling and handsome in their tuxedoes.

But during a wedding, it is not only the groom who is filled with mixed and happy emotions. There is someone else who is facing and feeling many complex emotions. The groom at least has a combination of feelings of excitement, happiness, sadness, love, and nervousness. But the other person is the bride's father.

The father of the bride during weddings is faced with the reality that is bittersweet and ultimately it dawns on him that his baby has grown up and is ready to move ahead. She will now have a new life with the man of her choice. The reality also strikes him that now he would be nudged sweetly in the second position in the title of the most important man in her life.

So, the speech made by the bride's father is a great way and an opportunity for him to accept in public and with a graciousness that his baby girl has bloomed into a woman. This is the best time for him to accept the groom formally and also his family as a part of his family. Whatever you write for your speech, just remember to let it out from your heart. Your heart would be your guide and see how everyone would be surprised when your speech turns out to be a memorable, heartfelt, and humorous address made to your daughter and her groom!

16 YOU ARE THE HOST OR MC

As per the tradition, the father of the bride has the most important role to play and that is of an MC, or master of the ceremony, during the wedding reception. As the master of ceremonies, the father has the task of introducing and giving thanks to the other speakers, for example, the maid of honor and the best man. But, there are few fathers who are not comfortable in playing or taking up this MC task. Therefore, it is completely acceptable forgetting someone from the family or even a friend to fulfill this task or role.

But mostly, the father of the bride is the MC; he has to play the part in the most ideal way. He has to play an organizer's role and see to it that the proceedings are on a roll as per the plan and time. As an MC he also has to set the ambiance, the mood, and atmosphere of the wedding reception. He has to make the celebration joyous and happy. A special note and care need to be taken that he should not make a mistake, especially putting himself as the evening's highlight and become the dominant person at the reception. The bride and groom are the highlights of the evening, it is the moment of their lives, and you had yours, so forget about getting any!

Professional MCs are hired by the family, so that there is better organization, hosting and setting of a good atmosphere. But all these come at the expense of the wedding budget and add up as extras. So, it is always a convenient idea that someone from within the family takes up the task of an MC and host the wedding reception.

As the host of the wedding, the father of the bride had to do a number of things in the deliverance of his speech. He has to offer acknowledgment, thanks, and gratitude to all individuals who have really helped out before and on the day of the wedding. He has to thank and show gratitude through his speech, from the caterers, minister, bridesmaids to the florists, for making the evening a perfect one and a dream come true for his daughter. Make a checklist and ask someone else to do a review before you make the speech so that nothing is left out or overlooked. As a bride's father, it is the day of joy and sadness at the same time. But you have to show it all through positive emotions.

17 IDEAS FOR YOUR SPEECH

These 30 topics and themes are some of the ideas that you can utilize in your speech as the father of the bride. You are the first speaker of the ceremony, so you don't want to sound lame or monotonous. Take these ideas and increase the quotient of your speech. You can talk on your wife's behalf too, mentioning her thoughts and insights related to the wedding, etc. So, be innovative and sound great by using these ideas in your speech.

Wishes and welcome:

1:- Start the speech as the father of the bride by briefly telling about yourself, since most of the people present would not know about you, especially the bride and groom's colleagues or friends.

2:- Welcome and give thanks to the guests for attending and sharing their presence on this day of your daughter's wedding, especially if there is no MC and you are acting as the host. Give special thanks to the guests who came from far off places to be present on this day.

3:- You can mention some incidents that are humorous in the reception and also try to highlight some moments, which you feel are beautiful and suit your speech. A single sentence would do.

4:- Give your happy wishes for the day or even the night.

Speech topics and ideas related to the bride

5:- In your speech, as the father of the bride, lend all your beautiful compliments to your daughter and say how beautiful and gorgeous she is looking, especially a lovely and elegant bride.

6:- Talk about your daughter to all the guests present, put your emphasis on the special and important relationship that the two share with each other. Tell them how much you love your daughter and how proud you are of her today. Also, let her know how much you love and care for her. Talk with affection and try not to use clichéd phrases, instead talk from your heart. You can tease her and make some funny comments but all should be done in the most courteous style, without hurting your daughter's sentiments and image.

7:- Tell about stories related to the bride, especially if they are silly and funny.

8:- Try to talk and reflect about the years prior to the wedding day and all in relation to the bride.

9:- Share with all about you and your better half's experience in seeing your daughter grow up into a lovely woman and stand as a bride in front of you.

10:- Share all your hopes and talk about all the highs and lows. But all these must be said in a gentle manner being the father of the bride and giving your speech.

11:- And as a part of your conclusion, you can include in your speech as the father of the bride and tell how proud you are today because of your daughter.

Speech related to the groom and your new son-in-law

12:- Share some funny stories in connection with the bride and the groom.

13:- Talk about the time when the groom was introduced to you for the first time and how did you break the ice and started to know each other. This will definitely work in your speech.

14:- Talk about the first impressions that you had regarding the groom and you can also describe the groom's looks.

15:- You can speak about the interests that each of you all share your relationship with one and another and also abut surprises that you faced as a father-in-law.

16:- Tell about the things that you were able to learn from the groom, in spite of being the bride's father.

17:- Tell about the happiness that he is able to provide your daughter with.

18:- Talk about his job, character, passions, hobbies, achievements, or even skills.

19:- In conclusion, the speech of the father of the bride, welcome him and tall how delighted you are to make him a part of your family from today.

20:- Welcome all to join you and your family together in accepting the groom and his family.

21:- Tell that how much eagerness you have in knowing him better. You can mention things that are common between both the families, along with thanking you's and gratitude in your speech.

22:- Being the bride's father, give your thanks via your speech to all who helped in making the wedding a successful one and show your gratitude for their generosity and help.

23:- Give thanks to the bride's mother or your wife and you can even thank the groom's mother, for all their efforts in the wedding organization.

24:- Don't forget to mention and thank the bridesmaids and maid of honor who have been all through with your daughter and compliment them on their looks, shower your thanks, and blessings for taking all efforts and giving their support to your daughter.

25:- Give thanks to the minister, clergywoman, or clergyman who had married your daughter.

26:- Thank all, from members of your family to friends as they have really helped in the wedding and its reception.

27:- Give special thanks to the florists, who made the venue look absolutely beautiful. You can say that everything in the hall, room, church, etc looks absolutely wonderful.

28:- If someone made a special contribution to the finance of the wedding, give thanks in a special way to them. You can say it in a humorous way too.

29: If your beloved is no longer present in this world, in her memory say few words. Tell all how much she would have been happy to see and be a part of this wedding

The conclusion to your father of the bride speech

30:- In the conclusion of your speech, raise a toast to the couple. Toast good health and a lovely future. I wish them both happiness and success for their future together and ask all to join you in making the toast.

18 YOU ARE READY TO ROCK AND ROLL

Speeches of the father of the bride are very solemn and sentimental moments of the wedding reception at the same time. It is more than a speech. It is all about a father's feelings for experiencing the feeling of letting go of his baby girl – the bride. Being the father of the bride, you have to overcome all these emotions and feelings and start preparing to give the speech as the bride's father on the day of your daughter's wedding reception. Make it a speech to be remembered, especially for your daughter.

The wedding day of your daughter is rather an emotional moment for any parent, especially fathers, as they are very close to their daughters. It is during this time that your daughter's entire life comes and works in your head, flashing all through. It hits as a reality that your daughter is all grown up now and she has made her choice. It is time to accept her choice and also accept the fact that she is meant for another man apart for you, who would be her life now. All these thoughts build within you and it is during your speech that you can release all the emotions. During your speech deliverance, you have to share your life experiences and also the positive experiences of married life, this should come as an advice to the newlyweds.

After the completion of the wedding ceremony, it is time for the reception and also for your speech, which would be the opening one. Wait up till all are seated and settled prior to making your speech. If there were a wedding planner, he or she would assist you with your speech. Your speech would be followed by the speech of the groom, the best man, and the speech made by the maid of honor.

Kick-off your speech, first by asking for everyone's kind attention. As it has been mentioned above, give a short self-introduction and then welcome all to the reception. Then continue the welcoming process by welcoming the family and friends of the groom. Once you have officially welcomed the family of the groom into yours, mention the greatness of the bride and groom, as a couple. Share a few words and talk about the ceremony and its success. Once all these points and welcoming are mentioned, start off your father of the bride speech. It is always good to start off with a little story. On the dependence of personal choice and preferences, you can tell a funny story or something emotionally related to the growing up days of your daughter.

A father of the bride's speech is incomplete without some praises and compliments given to your daughter and how lovely she looks like a bride etc. Let all know, especially the bride, regarding your nostalgia when the vows were being taken. Let her also feel proud of the thought that her father is feeling happy with her the most important decision of her life. Sharing stories in your speeches with the rest of the people present, as a father you can give some advice to the newlyweds for maintaining a happy and successful marriage. As an example, you can use your own married life and cite the happiness that you share with your beloved and see how your daughter light up and agree to it.

Always keep your speech, happy and interesting because it is a wedding party and not a funeral! You are responsible to keep it alive all through the night. Your speech is the beginning and it is also determining how the rest of the evening would be. You want to look experienced and proud. You must possess and air; after all, you are the father of the bride. And also the most important person in the subject's life! So, prepare your speech with all the guidelines, procedures, and lastly with simplicity.

Printed in Great Britain
by Amazon